MW01444700

Dark to Light
By Dean Ingram

Title ID: 4029839
ISBN-13: 978-1480127180

All rights reserved. No part of this publication may be reproduced, stored in a retrieval system, or transmitted in any form or by any means—electronic, mechanical, audio recording, or otherwise—without the written permission of the author/publisher. For further information, please visit www.deaningram.com or www.facebook.com/ingrambooks.

First edition published September 28, 2013.

Copyright: Dean Ingram

This book is dedicated to my brother.

May he rest in peace.

Addiction is a beast. It's a lifestyle that is rarely understood except by those who have experienced the darkest throes of its hopeless destruction. "Dark to Light" is dedicated to readers and their loved ones whose lives are or have been touched in any way by alcohol and drug addiction.

This book is not written by any psychologist, doctors or sponsored by a rehab facility or a recovery program.

It is written by a guy who started drinking at the age of 12. Over the next 43 years of his alcohol and drug addiction, he experienced multiple hospital stays, clinical depression, mental breakdowns, attempted suicides, rehabs, recovery programs, divorces and earned fortunes only to squander them away.

Meet Dean Ingram: "This book is about the darkest time of my life. A complete and total breakdown of my mind, my body, my emotions, my heart and everything I held dear. Taking my own life at that time seemed to me a good idea! This is the earmark of a terribly broken brain."

"Dark to Light" captures an intimate, deeply personal battle with alcohol and cocaine addiction which led the author to a profoundly creative avenue to document his emotionally charged turbulence - through poignant poetry and verse. Dean reveals the gritty barefaced truth of addiction, his courageous climb out of the rabbit hole of drugs and alcohol and his hard fought transformation to the man he is today.

With raw honesty, Dean offers realistic hope to those desperately struggling for a life of recovery, sobriety, strength and freedom from the beast.

Meet Dean Ingram

"Insanity is doing the same things over and over again and expecting different results."

As a reader of this work, you must keep your expectations low for my expectations certainly were in the writing and are still in the telling. My story is not unique, special or other worldly and there will be more on my story later in this book. I'm just a fellow who grew up without the tools to grow up. It took me 55 years of trying, succeeding, pissing it all away, digging myself out, trying again, succeeding and falling right back down the hole.

I think I first started writing verse and poetry in times of high emotion. I was trying to express things I couldn't express out loud. I was trying to find a way through some obstacle, imaginary or real, for which I had no map. I found after awhile that if I just let the thoughts come and let the pen write, that through the darkness of that particular emotion there would come answers that pointed toward the light.

I never realized at the time the poignancy of this exercise and how it would shape my life as I slowly descended into alcoholism and drug addiction accompanied by clinical depression. During the middle to late stages of that downward spiral, the verse and poetry came rushing back. I would isolate in my shop late at night, drunk, stoned, depressed and wondered to myself 'what event would occur that would help me stop this insanity?' And I would start writing.

The first few times were kind of raw and visceral but at the end, I did feel better. I never re-read them nor did I ever think that they would ever be released to the public. I was just a guy that found himself in a hole of his own making and had no tools to dig myself out save for this one thing – these poems.

As I kept writing night after night, I found I couldn't stop. It became easier and easier and although there were no sure answers, the poems always seemed to point towards hope in the end. A character would come to mind that may have been suffering the same as I and how would he get through? How would he find the light? And the words would just come.

I speak of this mostly because this work is about my last chapter of addiction, the darkest of my life. A complete and total breakdown of my mind, my body, my emotions, my heart and everything I held dear. Taking my own life at that time seemed to me a good idea! This is the earmark of a terribly broken brain.

I mentioned earlier that this work was never intended for the public eye and it wasn't my idea to make it available. I have not read this material in nearly 10 years but the person I love most in the entire world was convinced that it may help one of you or someone you know who might think that what they are going through is unique to them, that no one could possibly understand the depth of emotion that they are feeling and the impossibility of ever recovering from it. I have to say she has more faith than I.

So to you, the reader, I am humbled by your willingness to view this work. I do hope in someway that it may resonate with you or someone you know. I hope that the reader gains understanding of the similarities between us and not the differences.

Our similarities are, to me, significant.

Some may see this work and resolve that there is no way that we have anything in common, ok!

Others will see this work and think, "Oh my God, he's telling my story but I can't let anyone know."

Others still may read it, re-read it and find the one word or phrase that shines some light on their darkness and perhaps shows them that they are not alone, that there IS help.

And all one must do is be willing to ask for help and be humble enough to accept it.

The Experience

WHERE WAS I WHEN I GOT TO HERE

Where was I when I got to here
Not to notice the changes
And the things that divide
The questions unanswered
And the passion to hide.
Where was I when I got to here
I looked over my shoulder
And the road was so bare
Not a mark or a sign
That I had traveled there.

Where was I when I got to here
The road had turned
In the distance somewhere
And I could faintly feel it
Pulling me there.
But the pride of the man
Would not let me see clearly
And the end of the road
Hit so hard that it nearly
Shattered the man
I thought I could be
Up ahead in the distance
So far from reality.

Where was I when I got to here
In a dream there's a place
That will never know sadness
And a heart filled with love
That can overcome madness
It's a place that we long for
And desperately need
To be true to ourselves
And forget all the deeds
We've done in a way
We think can't be forgiven
It's a place where the heart
Is able to live

And as softly spoken
Encouragement finds us
We instinctively know
It's forgiveness that binds us.

QUIET HARBOR

Quiet Harbor
Quick lapping ripples
Surround the hull
But for the sound
There is no perception
Quiet Harbor.

UNCLE MERVE'S 70th BIRTHDAY IN ATLANTA

I just don't know, is all I can think to say. I don't want to come to any snap judgments. But five days out of my carefully woven element and my emotions are running wild. So I slipped the bond of that careful place I call home and tried my hand at being a part of a family I know very little about. I could see in the faces and the pictures everywhere that "Family" has bonded these people. Why have I not been able to be comfortable with the whole concept of "Family"?

Was my "Growing Up" so bad or did it just take me 53 years to start being or thinking unselfishly? Yes, that's the word. "Unselfishly". I can also see several veneers of justification shrouding it. So, if the lesson is to be "Be Unselfish" then it follows that the reward is "Family".

I always felt threatened the entire time I was growing up. I did not feel safe. I ran at every turn. Eventually I got tired of running and hid within. Only through the "Unselfishness" of my friends was I able to exist at all. That cocoon has lasted all these years. I have been generous but with selfish motives. I'm still hiding. I've tried not to threaten my children. But in keeping them at arms length from my madness and the fear of them suffering because of it, they have suffered from my selfishness. I have suffered for not recognizing the rewards in trusting to "Unselfishness".

Abundance is that which exists in the "Un-self". It is limitless. The "Self" has many walls and it continues to build them with every token of "Self". Every object that is for "Self" cannot be for "Un-self". And "Object" defined, is its own limit. Limits cannot exist in "Un-self".

Okay, so I'm a selfish bastard, a very scared selfish bastard. I can't believe I'm thinking all this but I'm glad to be writing it down.

Perhaps my cocoon is finished gestating. It's time may be near. Will the Butterfly be healthy? Is there still time to fix the flaws before it emerges unfinished and still running scared? A flower with no scent? An object with no light.? Still, silly selfish thoughts.

THE GLANCE

You can only look back
With a forward glance
If you expect to grow
And have another chance
To see what happened
Way back there
The defining moment
You became aware
That you're not alone
In this cosmic dance
That lets you look back
With a forward glance
But wherever I look
Both near and far
I know you're standing
Living, a shining star
An end, a beginning
No matter where we are
So let us look back now
We're free
To glance at the distance
As we
Find all the answers
As we look back
With a forward glance
And now in our hearts
It's time that we both
Can dance.

NO MO' SPLAININ' BLUES

No mo' splainin' baby
As I cried out loud
To see if you could see
The pale, frail man out there
Or the man I used to be

It could have been a while back
The doubt got started deep inside
God you got me cryin'
I'm sick and tired of tryin'
To find a place to hide

But I've had it up to here now
Don't you ask me to explain
You can listen to the storm outside
You can listen to the rain
You can listen to my heartbeat
As I sing this song in vain

I'm cryin' No Mo' Splainin'
I'm done tryin' to justify
Every move I'm makin'
You tryin' to catch me in a lie
I just can't keep from shakin'
I got the No Mo' Splainin' Blues

I'm cryin' No Mo', No Mo' Splainin'
I'm cryin' No Mo' Splainin' to you
I beg you No Mo' Splainin' Baby
I got the No Mo' Splainin' Blues.

FULL MOON
Emotion packed!

What do you think you're doing in here
In this solitary place
It's a dark excuse for living
In this self-indulgent space
Night after night you come here
What are you looking for
All the pieces of this puzzle
Were meticulously placed
What could you have forgotten
In the self-indulgent space
You sit alone here wondering
About what comes to mind
You write down a verse
And play guitar
Like you're looking for a sign
Some little thing, some honesty
Something you can't deny
But until that comes
Or you have the balls
To step into the light
Your nights will all be lonely
And you're days just turn to night
You play you're heart
With every stroke
You sing your songs to no one
You hope to hit
That magic note
That will capture the heart of someone
You're too upset
To take a stand
To unsure to make a move
As you wonder what you're doing here
In this solitary place
It's a dark excuse for living
In this Self-Indulgent place.

A SIMPLE MAN

I can't love you in the ordinary way
Too many walls are there to stay
I've gotten used to being who I am
Too complicated to be a simple man
I took refuge in a solitary life
Devoid of love, enveloped in strife
Too far over the other side
Perhaps this refuge is just simple pride
But I can't get back to how it used to be
And I can't remember the day that we
Took different roads so long ago
But we've traveled far and wide it seems
To end up in this place
This solitary, ordinary, Self-Indulgent space
So just let me stay and be myself
Let me love you through my deeds.

SANDS OF MIND

*I'm puzzled why so suddenly these feelings are pouring out
and why each time I'm drawn to ink it's almost like a shout
from somewhere way back in the "Sands of Mind".*

You've got to put your feet down one by one
Keep running hard into the sun
Put your mind at ease
Feel the freshness of the breeze
Don't worry if you suddenly stop
That time will pass you by
It's just the sands of time a blowin'
Giving to the sands of mind for knowin'
Don't get caught up in the sand of time
Their just drifting where they will
Give a purpose to the sands of mind
And the drifting sand will disappear
And open forth a way for you
To find yourself back on track and you
Gotta' put your feet down one by one
Keep running hard into the sun
Put your mind at ease
In the freshening breeze
No drift will ever bind you
You can see forever into
The waking memories along the way
And live the road of love
If it's love you get to live
Are you ever really in love
Or is it just loves journey
Look around at the road you're on
Love is there with every step you take
If it is true love that you seek
Don't ignore the journey
Take your time
Let it mold you
And teach you how to give
For love is the journey
If it's love you get to live.

LET ME SEE THE SUN

Let me see the sun
And let me follow
Give me now the moon
To rest my bones
Cause I'm feeling
Kind of weak
And hollow
On this road
Out here
So all alone
Well I set off on the right road
At a breathless, breakneck run
But I must have missed some signs
Along the way
So I stand here at the crossroads
It's plain as day to me
I could take the "shoulda' gone there"
Or the coulda' done that to this
And I woulda' loved to love you
Around that bend but for the things
I thought I'd miss
But it's the winding roads
Peeking out at me
From that dark road
Straight ahead
It's the one, I know
I can feel it
Could be lighter
Just around the bend.

WHO WOULD HAVE THOUGHT

Who would have thought
I couldn't stop it
Before it went too far
They would have never believed
I would let it go
And I've got to admit
That I didn't know
That a love could
Take you down so hard
To a Higher Place
Although it's far
From anything I've ever known
It seems to be
The way has been shown to me
With lighted pathways, sweet perfumes
A garden house with many rooms
It's crazy how my mind goes on
Just spinning thoughts of you
Let alone to write it down
In volumes, more than a few.

THE MILE OF LIFE

I've found my measure
On this crooked mile
A time for all to see
As we come down from the mountain
As the shore rises from the sea
No longer are we sightless
In a lonely, shrouded smile
Cause know we've found our measure
On this dark and crooked mile

The mile of life is calling
You can hear it on the wind
"I'll take you all in", it calls to you
Even though you may have sinned

So steady now as we go my friends
We're on this road to stay
And if you've found you're measure
It's not likely that you'll stray
It's time we come down from the hills
It's a time for us to be
It's time we bend our sails on
And venture back into the sea

The miles of life has brought you here
From a dark and distant past
As you traveled here it tested you
To see if you would last
It tore you're heart out many times
It gave it back ten fold
As you dodged and weaved
From place to place
Hiding out and getting old

So as you face the truth
And weigh the life
You've lived along the way
Try to understand that the mile of life

Is yours in all you say
The things you do and think
Are always going to bring you here
To the steps in the road called the mile of life
Find the measure, feel the pleasure
As the distance comes into view
It's the road they call the mile of life
And it's custom made by you.

GIVING YOU

I know I've not been giving you
The best I've got to give
Truth is, I've been lost
In another world
Trying to find out
How to live
I've been cruel to you in many ways
That I would not want for me
So let me thank you
For the time you gave
To let me just be me
There was a time I thought you might
Get up and say we're through
But you didn't and I've wondered why
Did you think at the time
That if you lie
To blind yourself
From what will be
That you'd end up
Right here right now
Standing in front of me
As I try to tell you
All that's true
What I know about being me
I'm not sure at all
Why I've faced this wall
But I know it's there for me
It's the one and only place
That will ever set me free
So we can face this thing together
If I could only let it be
I know I've not been giving you
Much call to think of me.

THE LIE

I'm writing songs like crazy
Like I thought I was going to die
I can't see past them
Which isn't all that bad
But I can't see past the lie
It's like all that's ever happened
Is laid down in a row
And it seems like all
I have to do is choose
Which way I want to go
But there's that lie
The one ahead of me
And off to either side
And I know that if I turned around
It would not try to hide
It's been tracking me a long time
And I haven't let it go
Not for lack of loving
But for something, I don't know
Maybe fear of all that fears itself
Is lurking just ahead
But I'll be damned before I let
This fear think that I'm dead
But that lie just sits there waiting
For something I just can't do
Which is kill the lie and let it go
And live my life with you
I guess it's been a long time
Since I've had a chance
To pen this many rhymes
But they just keep on pouring out
Trying to save my love
While there's still time
Cause I know my love might die
And they always lead to the question
What are you going to do about that lie.

LIVIN' LARGE

The reflection is not clear enough
To know which way to go
So we stumble on, rumble down
Humbled by the times.

We choose the way that's Large enough
To carry all the weight
We think we need to
Carry on and keep us
On the ground.

For if we fly too high
These days, the "Way"
Stops making sense
And "Livin' Large"
Is just some words
For "Life" in "Past Tense".

DARK TO LIGHT

It's a good day for thinking with the rain outside
A good time to listen to the wind in your heart
Where is it coming from, where is it going?
Why does it howl in my ears at times
And then becomes still?
At times the wind is warm and dry
At times it's cold and wet
But it's times like this
When the wind seem to cry out
"Stop me, slow me down
Don't let me fly through that hole in your heart
You've been long enough alone here
Listening to the wind"
So turn and face it strongly
Even though these thoughts seem fleeting
Whichever way it's coming from
It's just a form of greeting
If the wind seems cold sometimes
Just warm it as it passes through
If it seems too hot sometimes
Cool it as it caresses you
And when at times it seems just right
Enjoy it, feel it fill your heart
As forgiveness changes dark to light.

STITCHES

We talk as if the seams will burst
If we say just how we feel
The stitches in this love worn fabric
Are loose and fraying badly
And if the winds of change are strong
It doesn't matter who's right or wrong
As we stand on either side and sadly
Watch the fabric tear
And the stitches once so strong
Break and scatter in the wind
And we drift apart and wonder
Would a stitch of kindness
Have turned the tide
A stitch of love instead of pride
A stitch of respect
With an outstretched hand
A stitch of forgiveness and
It might have held for longer
It may have made us stronger
But the winds of change are blowing
And I can barely see you now
For the fraying ends of stitches
Scattered in the wind.

DIE WITH THE LIE

You're gonna die with the lie you told me
And you'll never tell me why
You left me standing in a pool of tears
They were flowing from my eyes

What did I do to make you leave me
For that short but killing time
I've been over and over the steps I've made
But I still can't seem to climb
Past all the dead ends I keep coming to
No life no love just lies
And that glowing, flowing pool of tears
That keeps falling from my eyes

You're gonna die with the lie you told me
And you'll never tell me why
All I'm left with is a lot of fears
That you'll do it again
Even if I try to love you
And let you live your lie
Let you find your own way back
But you may get lost and never come home
For all the love you fear I lack.

WINTERS COMING

Winters coming on
I can feel it
It's just around the bend
I can hear it
It's coming hard this way
I can see it
It's going to hit hard
Bang, here it is
And there it goes
I can feel the hole
It left in me
I can hear the wind
It's howling free
I can see the ice forming
Around my heart
And I can't do a thing about it.

IF I WERE TO GO TOMORROW

If I were to go tomorrow
What would I leave behind
That tattered shards of restless moods
Given to so many kinds
Of emotions that play Hide and Seek
In the shadows of my mind

If it weren't for the ones I love
I don't think I'd understand
The life that lay's before me
For all there is at hand
My family, our home
Our beautiful land
The purpose of this life, I feel
Is to live it to the end
To experience the ebb and flow
To navigate each bend
In "The River" so vast
As to hold all of time

Some vague idea of destiny
Too confusing to be born
You stumble into the daylight
You are tattered, you are torn
You're nerves are raw
But you're mind's alert
To the changes in the wind.

A TEAR IN THERE

Thank you for the time away
I think I'm back to stay
I've been gone so long so many times
I'm no good any other way
Where have I been? Well that's the thing
You know, it's not at all that clear
I've been lost and found so many times
I know it's been some years
Since I've been looking out this window
At the fences and the trees
The plants we started long ago
Out-lasted all of these feelings
The why'd I never go feelings
And my face is starting to show
The lines of so many sleepless nights
And in the corner of my eye, I know
There's a tear in there, it never goes away
But that's a story for another day
But anyway, thank you for the memories
I guess I can't really stay
But it was really good to see you
To see that smile on you're face
But you're frown just came back way too fast
And I guess I knew before I came
I could never make it last
But I had these feelings
Why'd I ever go feelings
But now I see it's time to go
I can see the distance in you're eyes
I can see the lines of many sleepless nights
I can see the hurt of all my lies
But the one thing I never saw before
In the corner of your eye
There's a tear in there, you say
It never goes away
But you're welcome for the memories.

NO, I'M NOT OKAY

No I'm not okay
But thanks for asking anyway
By any stretch of reason
No I'm not okay

I've got a heart full of tears
But I couldn't cry them anyway
By any stretch of loving
They were dried up by my fears

As my arms reached out
You didn't see me anyway
And suddenly they got heavy
As I filled myself with doubt

I used to be okay
And you asked me was there any way
By any stretch of reason
Did I think you're okay, too

Well I said that you're okay
And I asked you if there's any way
I could be you're man and be myself
And still remain okay.

I'VE TRIED TO WRITE MY STORY

I've tried to write my story
My thoughts in all their imagined glory
I've tried to fill in all the gaps
Between the longing and the tired taps
On the window as I looked outside
But I can't stop thinking
That I've missed the turn
It must have been a while ago
'Cause it's been awhile since I turned around
And it seems like miles to go
And the story keeps unfolding
As I watch it all go by
I keep on thinking I better get on board
Before I die.

PACE YOURSELF

Pace yourself. Let it unfold. You know in your heart it will be alright. You can still make it happen by controlling your emotions better. Try to stay focused on the Whole while completing each project. It is all connected. Each piece crafted for a lesson. Each no less important that the next; the courage to finish each piece and hold it in no less awe than the last until the Whole stands before you. This will be your test to yourself, of yourself, for yourself. Its completion is its own reward.

ON THE EDGE AGAIN

On the edge again. Familiar ground. Littered with unmet challenges, un-kept promises. Sorting through them once again. Don't stumble over that one. Watch out for the flying ones. They have no direction, no guidance, no faith, no purpose. They just bounce off each other, crashing into things. There is nobody there to watch over them. They have no order. Each in each others way. The only thing keeping them alive is the life you gave them just before you abandoned them to their own one dimensional world.

This being sick is very bad. I feel tingly and I can't breathe very well. I can't eat and my brain is shutting down. Hope I get better soon. I have moments when I feel okay and moments that I'm sure I'm going to have a stroke or heart attach. I'm throwing my life away. I'm trying to kill myself. I have created such aloneness that I fear my only refuge is more aloneness. I better figure out why and deal with it. I've retreated so far that I don't belong anywhere. I though I'd found God. I did. What happened?

SPINNING TOWARD THE DARK SIDE

Losing focus. The trap was sprung. All the fears I've had for years became real. Regrets in my face and a hole in my heart. I am ashamed. There are brief glimpses of my end because of this. Peering into my inability to live with the mess I've made of things. I have no self respect left. I had a plan! I was working up the courage to be a man. It was still taking shape. Quiet time spent figuring out the steps. The blind faith that kept telling me it was the right thing to do. The desire to get up each day and know that my purpose was clear. The knowledge of the sacrifices to its end was easier to carry. The new goal was fresh. Worth fighting for. Not an easy plan. Maybe not even a smart plan. But it woke me up. Things became clearer. Then I came face to face with a loss that I could not bear. I grabbed hold of it for dear life and in that moment I lost everything. There is nowhere I can go to escape the shame, guilt, sorrow and pain. I know this is the hell I feared the most. Silently unable to accept love for the stress of my sins. Setting aside all passion for fear of its power and my weakness in its spell. So as this dialogue continues I pause and wonder what I'm most upset about. My weakness. I understand it but have difficulty avoiding it. I don't know what will happen but I know I'm scared to death. I know I can't keep dodging the bullet. I've got to stop myself. The weakness is the power I have. I'm unable to keep it focused. I cannot harness it. It wants to do good but sometimes it seems easier to just let it go and see what happens. It rarely turns out well. So now it occurs to me that I'm being selfish. The person who bears the brunt of this soap opera is taking the heat as I sit here downing in my pity pool. I feel pathetic. I can't get away from myself. Reason enough for the end to come. I rather liked the thought of becoming like my father. There was a certain security in working on things in my shop. Shining up the bike. Letting go of the boat and all the guilt that went with it. Building my village in my mind. It's more than I can hope for and certainly more than I deserve. Could so useless a soul find salvation? What shape would it take? I have no honor. It is too much to bear. My inner voice calls out, "Don't do anything drastic". I'll listen for awhile. Waiting is the worst. I could end my pain now. I'll wait awhile. Maybe the power is just an illusion. Maybe I'm just another classic fool with delusions of grandeur and my reality can't cope with it. Although my reality from this point of view looks pretty weak. Vanity! How does it play into each piece of the downfall? I'm just in everyone's way. But my demise would only compound the carnage I have created. Dilemma! The more I write while in this mood, the more bad things I come up with to say about my life. I've got to save the good and play it out. Let go of the bad and pray I know the difference.

THE FLOW HAS STARTED

It seems each time I sit and write
It all tries to come out at once.
To fit it into place right now
I'd have to say that the flow has started.
If I keep it up I can train myself
To feel the flow at will.
Don't let it scare you.
Let it guide you. Maybe!
I don't know if I'm ready
To let anything guide me.
Yes, even after all the
Verse you gave me
I'm afraid of letting go
And even more afraid not to.

EMOTIONAL HIBERNATION

Emotional hibernation
Sleeping through
The dark days of winter
Sleeping through
The hazy days of life
Hiding away
From all that is
To avoid the small,
Hurtful things
Living life crippled
By that which you avoid.

I'LL LET FATE BE MY COMPANION

I'll let fate be my companion
I'll watch as trouble turns away
I'll let fate be my companion
And dive into a better day

I'll let fate be my companion
Lonely nights will be no more
For with fate as my companion
I won't be lonely anymore

I'll let fate be my companion
And serendipity be my guide
I'll clear out all the cobwebs
And try to show a better side.

YOU'VE GOT TO TAKE STOCK!

Okay! You keep getting glimpses. You've got to take stock! Inventory, if you will. List all the things you are involved in and then set them in order of importance. You are living too thin. Although the good moments are really good, the time in between is without direction of any kind, save the pull of the chaos you've created around you. And you resist even that without a higher thought to keep you going.

"I want to believe in something". When it comes down to it there is only God or me. Would that one or the other make the difference and give me lasting focus? Alas, my heart tells me, there can only be one. A home base, a place of comfort and confidence that I can take with me anywhere. Godself, perhaps? More likely, God.

TWO SHADOWS OF ME

I walked out on the porch last night to take my dog for a walk. The spot lights were on and as I stepped to the edge of the deck the lights cast two shadows of me: one to the right and one to the left. It struck me as very odd. Which shadow to follow? I wanted to follow the one to the right. It seemed to be the clearest. The one to the left looked more faded but was calling just the same. It was a compelling moment. I went right. The frequency of these moments is alarming and comforting.

WINDS OF CHANGE

So I let go of reason and was cast adrift
On the tide of emotion, the winds of change
The stormy sea was waiting for me
Almost as if I'd been there before
Perhaps in better days I'd been there
Long before the storm
I had danced across the wave tops
And I'd heel into the wind, what fun
I'd dropped the anchor in a sheltered cove
And lay there napping in the sun
\and you were right beside me
Such a rich life we had won

But as I pause to think about that time
A tear falls in the tide of emotion
Another is cast to the winds of change
And again the stormy sea is waiting
For my life, my heart to re-arrange

Would reason take me back there
Would the tide of emotion then be calm
And the winds of change be still
Would the sea settle into a steady roll
And what of love on this sea of mine
Where has it drifted to
I can't help but think I've lost it
And as adrift as I am now
I'm not sure I'll run across it
In this whirling tide of emotion
In these howling winds of change
\on this stormy sea that's calling me
To where the love and reason dance as one
In that sheltered cove lying in the sun

No more will emotion rage and fume
No more will the wind blow cold
No more will the sea cast it's fury on me
No more will my anchor refuse to hold

So please take away these feelings
And let them find their way
Give the strength to steer this ship
To a home where I can stay.

IF I SAILED BACK IN TIME

I sailed back in time to a harbor
That I'd been to a long time ago
It was everything that I remembered
When I was there a long time ago
But I cast away from that harbor then
And sailed a course of my own
But those anxious moments
That turned into years
And the desperate farewells
That turned into tears
They've come back around
With no rhythm or rhyme
Dancing just out of reach
A step out of time
I can see it as clearly
As if it was now
If I sailed back to that harbor
That I'd known such a long time ago
Would I be ready to see
All that's troubling me
And let that harbor of dreams fall away
And those beautiful scenes be replaced by
Sailing now, this minute to that harbor
Racing headlong into the storm
Digging deep as the moment takes hold of me
Feeling all there is just to be free
Finding all the answers in a simple prayer
Please don't let time be just about me
As I sit here letting these words pill forth
I'm wondering where they were born
I pause just a moment to catch my breath
And again I'm off in the storm
Of phrases that just come to mind
Almost as if their speed goes straight to the page
Without the pen -- Fascinating!

RUNNING HARD AWAY

Well, I can't explain the things I do
Well, I guess I could if I wanted to
But I'm running hard away from you
As far as I can go
I looked at us in the light of day
And I peeked at where we'd turned
And I watched you go the other way
I felt the fire, God it burned
And I stood there for a moment
As I wavered in the light
Then suddenly I saw it
I was reeling from the sight
Of that Lie that cut into my heart
And took away my light.

9-11-2001

There are no words now, nor, I fear, in the future that can comprehend what the world has witnessed today. Our country that we love and love to hate has been attacked. Fear has been realized. Fears we hadn't suspected. Fears that will set civilization on a course no one can know. Fear beset by egos that can and will retaliate, fears that will generate a calling, galvanizing those fearful. Will clearer minds prevail or will they be as galvanized against the fear? Don't be afraid. Fear is the enemy. Anger is the weapon.

9-12-2001

We are burning candles for you
Though we don't know who you are
We have sat awake each night since then
Watching, hoping, weeping, reviled by the pain
For some that morning will never end
The first thing they see when they awake each day
The last thing they feel as they kneel and pray
The hours between, that face in the crowd
You know that you know them and you call out loud
Then you realize they're not the one you thought
And it hits you like a shot
Those faces shall no more grace this world
They have answered for their time
No more burden cast upon them
No more fear shall haunt them
In their moment before, they know their fate
And resolved, they answered the call
How brave were they.
How brave were they all.

9-13-2001

It seems strange tonight to hear jets overhead after two nights of silence. When I took my dog out for a walk on Tuesday and Wednesday night, I looked to the North where they usually stack up waiting to land. There was nothing. No planes anywhere. It's hard to tell now, if the sound of planes winging is reassuring or not. The images of the last few days have been horrifying.

Knowing your enemy is a powerful weapon. They knew we would obsess. They knew we would turn our media, unrestrained, to the grim task of reporting every detail of this horror. They knew that the media would ram it down our throats playing the horror over and over again to make sure that no one would forget the images. If the lowest common denominator of horror is common place, then, naturally it must be reported endlessly. I have shunned the thought of the images that will be shown tomorrow as they dig deeper and start to uncover the carnage beneath the soot, the dust, the pulverized concrete, the twisted beams, glass turned to molten goo, the silence, the unspeakable. But it must be shown. We must react to it in our own way. It's time is now and we are here to witness the unfolding of History.

Have Prophets foretold these deeds? Have they seen to the souls they knew would be set free? Have they challenged the notion that we have been here before? Or has it finally shown them that it all happens now. If you have a moment to reflect on the past, do you not bring the past into being again?

9-14-2001

In times such as these many things shall be spoken
In rage and confusion, our prayers but a token
To that which surrounds you
We must call on each other to brave this new world
As it emerges around you
What corner of hope have we reserved for this time?
This time we are called on to be

All of things we've put off for so long
For chasing the shadows of "Me"
I now sense a difference each day that I wake
The depth of all there is to see
The fog as it lay's in the pasture
The morning sun climbing above the trees
Watching my Dog as she sniffs the air
And leaves tracks in the dew on the grass
The spider web laced in backdrop
For the morning to Be.

WHERE ARE THE ANGELS

Where are the Angels spoken of
Foretold of times like these
I believe they are here now working hard
Doing the work of Mortal Men
For Mortal Man was not meant to see
In the darkness of the ruins
God, those images haunt me still
Those Angels clothed as Mortal men
Have a job they must fulfill
As they keep digging in the dust below
We dig deep into our hearts
But never deeper shall we dig
Than those Mortal Men dressed as Angels
Digging in the dark.

MORNIN' AFTER BLUES SONG

I got some whiskey
I got some wine
I got some time to kill just realizin'
What I lost was never mine

I've been a fool all these years
I can't say that I ever knew
What this life was like with clear eyes
What this life was like with you

I've been blinded by my selfishness
I've been wanderin' in the mist
Of that Mornin' After Blues song
Of that mornin' after kiss

I got some whiskey
I got some weed
I got some time to kill just takin' stock
Of the things I really need

But there's so much clutter in the way
Of the wants that turned to deeds
That took away my clear eyes
That took away what was left of me

And I'm still blinded by my selfishness
And you have vanished in the mist
Of that Mornin' After Blues song
And that hasty mornin' kiss

Of all that whiskey
Some wine and weed
Surrounded by forever wants
That turn into forever deeds

I got some whiskey
And that's all I got that's mine
Except the time that I've got left to kill

So I'm sittin' here just killin' time

Singin' that Mornin' After Blues song
You know I got the blues
Singin' that Mornin' After Blues song
For you.

JUST AN OLD FOOL

Just an old fool running out of time
Trying to hang onto what I once thought was mine
In my youth I was daring
As I challenged each day
As I sent it to fit my perception
But the days just kept coming
And I tired with age
And my daring was replaced with reflection
Of days bending lies to my will then to theirs
Of the memories of daring and putting on airs
And try as I might to be bold in the light
Of those days as they're passing me by
No matter how I try to replace them
I'll never be near them again
Those daring days of youth for me
Are just the strains of my memory.

NO ONE THAT YOU KNOW

No one that you know is a casual friend
They are here as part of your life
They test the moods you wake up with
They lend a hand when your world turns to strife
They may cause you to wonder
They may stir up your fire
They may hold all the hidden clues
To unlock your fondest desire
So be careful not to judge them
Let them be who they will be
Be thankful that you shared with them
And will always have that memory
We can't always take the right road
In our daily dash at life
Mistakes are made by everyone
As part of the beauty of learning
They set into play
All the twists of the day
They can balance a heart
That burns with yearning
For events that keep perspective fresh.

BROKEN

You've broken some buildings
You've broken our hearts
And you've broken the backs of a few
But our spirit has risen with strength anew
As your beliefs are foreign to us
Our beliefs are foreign to you
You've taken a step out of time for us
You've caused some worry and doubt
But the path we are on is a long one
And we're a lot closer to figuring freedom out
But I know this for certain
That our dream is still alive
And the backs you have broken are just a token
Of the backs we have to defend our beliefs
Which, no doubt, are as real as yours
But have no doubt they are real to us
Why haven't you stepped forward by now
Your beliefs trying to justify
The cold hearted malice
That your deeds do imply
Come out of hiding take your stand
Face up to what you have done
The only thing taught
By the terror you've wrought
Is that soon you will be undone
Look into your heart
For the prayers that were lost
Find them, keep them
Follow them through
The time you are blessed with
The time you have used
Have come to this time
In your life as you knew
Just words on paper
Or a waving of sabers
To the fear you are facing
To the delicate lacing
Of dreams you have dreamed

The ones that you've kept
As they are woven together as one.

I WANT TO SAIL

I want to sail to an Island
And be somebody else for awhile
I've lost track of the track I was riding
All I need is some warmth and a smile
But it seems I've worn out my welcome
For the carrying on that I've done
And in my heart of hearts
I've lost trust of friends that I love
Thinking that love was just lust in the sun.

SOLACE IN ALCOHOL

I've taken solace in alcohol
My dreams of youth so far away
Did I dream then
Or this dream now
And still my youth is so far away
Perhaps dreams are woven tighter
As youth slips away and time goes by.

I DO WHAT I CAN DO

Well, I get up every morning
And I do what I can do
I go to bed every evening
And I dream
And while I'm doin' what I'm doin'
If I pause to look ahead
I can see the light
As it's streamin' in
I can hear the call of the wild
I can see myself sailin' on the wind
I can see myself as child
With dreams of everlasting
With goals forever more
With a passion for the life I live
As I open each and every door
Where is that child when I need him most?
Where did the everlasting go?
Where are the goals forever more?
What of the passion and the life you live?
Can you see your dreams in those around you?
Can you find the strength to forgive?

RHYTHMS AND RHYMES

The stuff I just wrote
Started out kind of different
But I let it just wander along
It's funny sometimes
How the rhythms and rhymes
Suddenly turn into a song
I just try to get quiet
And let it pour in
As it dances its way
Through thick and through thin
These words, you see,
Are just venting for me
They come and they go
With the mood
But as the pages turn
My heart starts to yearn
For more words to tell a story
For more dreams to fill the night
For more time to spend
Discussing thoughts with my pen
Of living life with no end
Though the end seems near.

AS MOMENTS TURN INTO YEARS

There's no magic tonight
As I fumble with the strings
I've spent the magic on yesterdays
On less cerebral thoughts
On more material things
And so the moments
Transform each moment
Into a rhythm I can't hear
And I find myself
Not much further along
As moments turn into years.

THE FINAL END OF YOU AND ME

You tell me there's no way to see
The final end of you and me
But I don't know where I'm going to turn
If I don't just turn around now
As I turn around I can see the light
It's still shining there for me
Yes I can see it now as I'm drawing near
All this time I couldn't see
As I turn around I can hear the call
Of the hearts I left behind
They are just as pure as the day I left
All these years I've been so blind
If I turn around now
My running days are through
My crying days are gone
And I turn around now
And this moment starts anew

As I turn around now
I can see the light
I can hear the call
It's still shining there for me
I can feel the warmth of you
As I fumble back through all my dreams
I can see where it began
And you tell me there's now way to see
The final end of you and me

And I know I've got to turn around
To find my way back somehow
Because I don't know where I'm going to turn
If I don't just turn around now.

GIVING, TAKING, THINKING, LOVING, FAKING, DRINKING

The sun goes down much sooner now
Leaving sun-starved and wanting
These days so precious
The memories so haunting
I've been working on my music
Pretty hard of late
And I've been staying out
Much later than I should
It seems I've got to be
A part of everything
Giving, taking, thinking
Loving, faking, drinking
Waking all those feelings
That have slumbered for so long

Don't you wonder
In your lonely thoughts
Where it all began
Have you built it up
As an impenetrable wall
Do you really think
It's all or nothing at all
Can you reel it in now
Can you call it back
Can you see beyond the haze
Or are you just going to stand there
And let your world pass you by
Never lifting yourself
Out of the daze
Will you find your love
Or is it lost forever
Or is it dangling in between
This gap I live and call a life
I know I could love
If I could stop saying IF.

A FEW FINAL THOUGHTS

A few final thoughts
As I ready to leave
As I put this day to rest
Have I given it an honest try
Have I given it my best
Did I honor those that went before
Did I guard the ones to come
Did I love the ones that love me now
Did I help myself be myself
Did I try to overcome all the errors
That I made the day before
Did I try to dry those tired eyes
And the tears I caused to flow
And the relish in the friends I've made
And the friend they've made in me
It's a long, hard road to honor
But a friend can always see
How to be a friend
In bad times or good
A friend is a wonderful thing to be
Just a few final thoughts
A clean palate as I paint this song
Will black be the background or shall it be white
It matters in the long run
The moods I will paint
Some shiny and bright
Some void of light
Some with so much color and richness of life
Some are waiting for just the right shade
Of confidence to take away all the strife
But nothing stands still for very long
And to capture it within a song
Don't color it with doubtfulness
Don't try to shade it from view
The reds of rage and passion
The blues of ache and need
But the greens of comfort
Find their way to the place I first saw you.

THE DOUBTS

Every time I get some time
To spend some time with you
The doubts come rolling down the hill
The fears blow cold, my heart stands still
Then you see through me and deep into me
And you carry me away
And we share our time
With the time we have
And love and laugh away the day
But a day seems closer somehow
Seems fuller in the end
Than the wanting of the moments yet to be
The richness of the time we spend
Are they really stolen moments
Are they really meant to hide
From the light you bring into each day
To keep me from the Darker Side.

AND WHAT OF YOUR SHIP, LAD?

And what of your ship, lad
She languishes in the harbor
The harbor of your childhood
The harbor of your dreams
The harbor that you look to even now
I can see her lines, still graceful
Powerful, under full sail
Each wave another joy
She dances and springs
She settles into a rhythm
Miles slip by under her
The hard miles I've logged on land
Slip away as if I've cut the strings
So what of your ship, lad
Will you reduce her to memories
Trade her for excuses
Put her off for your indecision.

RUNNING DOWN THE ROAD

I saw you running down that road
I saw you running fast
It looked as if you were running to me
Until you ran right past

I don't know where I got the notion
That you were ever looking for me
I was sure that I had your devotion
But looking now, it's plain to see
That you're just running down that road

Don't you ever pause and stare
At that man there standing
By the side of that road
The man that used to care

So I guess I'll see you out there
Running down that road so fast
But I'll only see you for a flash
Cause now I've got to run
Man, I've got to dash

Perhaps someday our roads will meet
When our running days are through
Now we're faster than that road can take
For two runners going nowhere near
The love that road could make.

THE CALL OF THE WILD

I'm calling on the Call of the Wild in me
To set me right, to help me see
This isn't a game we're playing here
This isn't the time to be letting fear
Call all the tunes you dance to
So let your wild self get a hold of you
And show you how to survive
Cause as your wild self
You'll always be yourself
You'll always be fresh and alive
And as your wild self tames a better you
And your passion returns to your heart
It'll be your wild self that you turn to
The one that's always shown you the way
And the lessons that you've gathered
Will finally see the light of day
It's your wild self that you must be
Before your self runs out of time
Let your wild self be your wild self
And just let yourself be you.

IS THE FOG CLEARING?

Is the fog clearing?
I so wanted to just reflect
This weekend away on the boat
Safe and warm, familiar
Alone but not lonely
Why is it so different?
On the boat?
On the water?
I guess it's the feeling
That little, if any bad news
 Is likely to come knocking
And then there is sailing
Trimming her to fly free
The smell of the salt
The waves as they peel off
The bow and swell astern
The oneness of so many things
Brought together to sail
To be sailing
There is little time to reflect
Only time at time's pace
Here in the wind
Here on the water
Here on the boat.

LOVE

Love is the absence of wanting
And the fulfillment of needing
Because love is everything
Love and want will disappear
Love and needs are fulfilled
It seems so simple
If everything you do is based in love
Then love becomes the process which
Produces love as a result
Nothing can defy it
Nothing, in the end, can challenge it
You may be bruised, you may be hurt,
But love will guide you, keep you,
Heal you, set you free.

CHARLOTTE'S FIRST BIRTHDAY

It's hard to calculate the effect this dog has had on me. She has kept me from going too far and has filled countless hours of my aimless days. Healing. How long does it take? Charlotte was sent here to help me build a family where a huge hole lived in me, the hole where our family used to be. She gives us little glimpses of sharing, of caring and of Love. She breaks my heart when she is sick or hurt. If I watch her closely, I can feel what she feels. I can see what she sees. It is a very strong connection that began the very first time I saw her. "Charlotte" was her first word to me. "Love" was the second and "Give" was the third. A heavy load. I'm thankful to be chosen to bear it. Doubt gives me pause for my worthiness to answer the call. But Love and Selflessness ring loud and true and doubt be damned.

HAPPY BIRTHDAY CHARLOTTE!

WHAT PATH?

What path, this
As I stare at a landscape unfamiliar?
Dare I step there?
Have I not already begun?
Has this turn come at
The expense of passion
You have used as
The fuel to wish it true
Will it not take that much
Passion and more
To keep you on your way?
Passions shared with love
Is love for who ever may be
Close enough to share
But the one you must
Turn to will know these passions
And not be afraid, only
If you are not afraid.

FOR THE FEAR OF LEARNING

For the fear of learning
Much too much
I crashed into the wall
My work was simple
Day by day
Conquering demons
As I dreamed them all
Putting words in their way
Walking slowly in their shadow
Until that one streak of light
Found me, woke me, made me see
Beyond those pockmarked walls of fear.

FAR AWAY SAILOR

I've been living the life of a sailor
I need to live my life on the sea
I've worked on many a whaler
I've been away as far as can be
Far away is where I've made my life
Never far but never near
Far away somewhere
Toward the setting sun
Far away is where my life has gone
Watching sails in the sunset
Seeking favor in a storm
Working hard to keep my ship up
From all the weather she has borne
Thinking hard of ways
To continue my days
Far away on the horizon
Far away and never back
Far away is my home now
It's where I've made my life
Far away somewhere
Toward the setting sun
Far away is where my life has gone
But now it brings me here
To sing this song
This song of a life of a sailor
This song of a life on the sea
I know it's away from the ones I've loved
But I know that it's home to me.

THESE MOODS

These moods that bring me here again
Thinking, shrinking, clutching my pen
Wasting ink of tired phrases
Line after line, page after page
Slowly rising from the haze
The light begins to shine
The sun begins to warm
To melt the fog and these moods
That find me here again.

IF YOU GO A WANDERING

If you go a wandering
It gets hard to come back home
The love you once knew
Becomes shattered it seems
The love you once knew
Becomes nothing but dreams
Of the love that can
Bring you back home
So think of the love
You have in your life
Think of the love
That you've taken
And think long and hard
Before walking out of your yard
Because if you go a wandering
It gets harder to come back home
And the love you once knew
Becomes tattered and worn
And the hearts that you took
Become shattered and torn
You wander the streets
To find shelter
From the storm
That you left in your wake
As you blazed right through
The love you once knew
And the hearts you chose to forsake
The moment you went a wandering
Did you ever pause to look back
Did you look down the road
At the dust and the rain
Did you ever look into the eyes
Of the ones that you love
Couldn't you see the love there for you
Why did you think that you had to go
As you wandered away from the ones that you know
Wasn't one life enough to be blessed with
Did you think you had to have more

So here you are still a wandering
You know it's too late to go home
All for the sake of wandering
You will always be alone.

THE LAST DAYS OF SUMMER

The last days of summer
Have come to this
A random day perhaps
But it marks the end of growing
And reflection takes hold of time
A new season, new colors
The greens of summer fade
Slowly at first
Change to yellow
Then burst, pastels
And fall one by one
Two by two
The leaves start falling
A carpet on the ground
A multitude of mood
Lots of fun to kick around.

THE ONE YOU KNOW YOU'LL BE AGAIN

Most songs talk of life
Some talk of living
Some of love gone bad
Some talk of forgiving
But let this song
Keep bringing you
Closer to the truth
Closer still to
The one you've been
Lifetimes before
The one you know
You'll be again
The one who knows
The way back home
When you're out there
A bit too far
The one who prays
To God at times
The one who wishes
Upon a falling star.

LET YOUR HEART SING

Let your heart sing
Let it ring true
Your mind will follow
If you'll just be you
Always believe
In the power of love
Always believe in your heart.

HE SPOKE TO ME

He spoke to me of attitude
He questioned my resolve
I said to him the platitudes
Will never, ever solve
The myriad of questions
They've put before your throne
The attitude I carry
Is the only thing I own
It's something very close to me
I don't speak of it often
It is just what I am
And it helps me to soften
The edges of the fear
That I see in your eyes
The things that you claim
Things you call your prize.

The hardest thing about being a human
Is letting ourselves be human.

A RICHNESS

There is a richness to life
That often escapes us
As we ponder the seeming
Hardships and joys
It seems to lie in the
Deepest part of the heart
Waiting for its discovery.

Can you?
You Can!
Will you?
You Will!
Shall you?
You shall!
May you?
You may!
Are you?
You Are!
Must you?
You Must!

RUNNING

Can I stay ahead of the thunder
Can I stay ahead of the rain
I've no time left to wonder
About the source of all this pain
But I've got to stop running
Cause I'm just worn out
And for all my running
I can't stay ahead of the doubt
So I keep on running
With the thunder at my back
And the rain erasing everything
And covering my track
But I've just got to
Stop the running now
I'm not sure why
And I'm not sure how
But I know if I keep running
I know if I don't stop
I'll die in place while running
Running to reach the top
I'm not sure at all
But I might be running
Because I just can't stop.

Confidence is a steady hand
Your heart open
Your mind focused
Your purpose clear
What must it be like?

ANGER

If anger, given wings, could fly
Then would love bring it back to the ground?
And once you tie and tether it
Knowing full well
You may yet have to weather it
Should you give it wings again.

WHERE DO YOU TURN TO

Where do you turn to
Once you've turned around
And you're still running
Down the same old path
And if you stopped running
And looked straight ahead
Or over your shoulder instead
Which view would be you
As you stood there
Catching your breath
Could you go any
Direction you choose
I'm sure that you could
And you happily would
If only the others
You would not have to loose.

THEN AND NOW

There seems to be an art
To the seamless transition
Between then and now
Some folks are gifted
And seem to know how
But the problem I'm facing
Between then and now
Is
What happens next?

THE CALL

The call, it seems has come at last
I can hear it riding up so fast
I'm not sure this time that it will last
Any longer than before
I can hear it calling out to me
Saying this is your time to be free
But I'm not so sure I can free myself
Any better than before
Cause I've been away so long now
That I don't remember me
And I've lived so many lives along the way
But if I could live one life again
I know I couldn't stay away
And I'd end up on this dusty trail
Thinking I can hear you calling
I can hear you riding up so fast
I want to ride with you
But I'm broken and I'm falling
And even though I hear you calling
It won't ever be what it used to be
And the voices that were calling
Start to fade at last
And you're left with
What you started with
No better than before.

THE STORY

If you were to tell me your story
Do you know where it would start
Would you count the times you faltered
When you could not save your heart
And the times when you were overjoyed
Just before you fell apart
Well, you're writing your own story
Every chapter, every phrase
You can turn the page
To a different age
You can spin the lines around
But don't get lost in the story
Don't forget who wrote the lines
And as you're writing your own story
You're the one who owns these times
And you can't erase the lines you wrote
But I'm pretty sure you'll find
Over time the lines come easier
As you settle into your style
You're more comfortable with who you are
You've been at this for awhile.

JUST BEFORE THE FALL

What was it that you saw
Just before the fall
Did it matter then
Does it matter at all

Well, you've fallen on some hard times
And your world is upside down
And you haven't felt apart of it
Cause you're always feeling down

Well, it might have been your pride
That you saw that night
Just before you hit the wall
And you woke up suddenly
To find you'd lost it all

I guess we both were just dreamers
And our dreams somehow fell apart
And I lost my way to forever
I lost my way to your heart

Can we find our way back
To the dreams of before
Can we find our way back at all
Can we dream our way
Back to that distant place
Can we find our dreams
After The Fall.

LETTING GO

Sometimes it's just about letting go
Sometimes I've got to be free
So before this day is over
And another catches up to me
Before I say my prayers tonight
Before I let my soul take flight
Let go, just let go
Just take a chance
Do a little dance
And let go, just let go.

TRUST

She trusts me, I gotta follow through
You say you trust me
But I don't trust you
Trust, yeah, trust in me now

Trust, if I give it to you
Where you gonna take it to
Who you gonna show it to
Trust, yeah, trust in you now

Trust, where you gonna get more
Once I run out of it
Where you gonna find a fool to
Trust, yeah, trust in the lord now

Trust, it's the only thing I'm clingin' to
If I let go and don't follow through
I'll never find another way to
Trust, yeah, trust in you and me now

Trust, where's it gonna take us to
If I give it all to you and
Do just what I said I'd do with
Trust, yeah, trust in you now

Trust, stand a little taller now
It's all about how far we'll go
To make a stand and follow through with
Trust, yeah, we're getting down to it now

Trust, alright, can I trust myself
Can I just put that to rest
No, you say, it don't work that way
Cause every day they're gonna try to test your

Trust, yeah trust in me
Trust, yeah trust in you
Trust, yeah, trust in the Lord now

Trust is the word worth fightin' for now. Trust!

YOUR STORY

There is much sadness in your story
A hollow rattle in your voice
It seems to me in the telling
You're just echoing your own choice
So tell your story no more
And fill that hollow space
You're just one forgiveness away
From a deep and richer place
And a much more beautiful day
If you carry your past
The memory will last
Whether bad or good
So leave the sad stories behind you
And let the good life take you away
Let the wonder of what is before you
Help you be yourself today.

I'M SOMEONE ELSE

I'm not my own self anymore
I'm someone else
But I don't know who
I gave it all away
To a dream gone bad
And I'm someone else
And I don't know who
Which way is the way back
To where I need to be
And is that way
The way back to you
If I found you again
Would you know who I am
Cause I'm not my own self anymore
I'm someone else
Maybe you know who
It's hard to find a way
Back from nowhere else
And I'm not my own self anymore.

FIGHTING IT SO HARD

Always the question of whether I want to be be drawn further into the web. Why am I fighting it so hard? Fear? Selfishness? Commitment?

I'm so afraid of choosing a direction that it's made me immobile. Seems like I've got so many things pulling me in so many directions, lots of uncertainty and just plain being scared that a certain amount of shame accompanies that level of fear. A multiplier of sorts. It's always the same. Spiraling down. Why can't I stop it? Is it a single thing that keeps me apart from joining, committing, working to accomplish something worth doing, or is it a collection of character flaws that come and go like the seasons? Small nodes of negative energy that if collected in enough supply just wipe out all other forms of energy I may possess. I feel as if I've broken down.

Most of my energy spent just keeping the shell alive. Not enough energy left to rebuild, to heal, to put enough issues to rest to start climbing out. Let alone figure out which direction to climb.

It can't be that difficult? Why don't I get it? Is this normal? I don't think so.

I'VE LOST MY WAY COMPLETELY

I've lost my way completely. No focus. Filled with fear. Doubt. Silent rage at myself for knowing the way, being held by the hand. Feeling that I can't even say the word 'joy' because it's just not there anymore. What was Grand is no more.

I was charged with keeping it all alive but I didn't want to live. I thought I found God. He saved me. Didn't ask for anything. Just showed me the way. It was mine to lose and I lost it. All the things going on in our lives comes under scrutiny today when RG gets home. My life will not stand up to much scrutiny.

I am the worst of men. I could expect no less of those I've touched. I cannot continue to live a lie. To be so many different personalities has worn me out. Too many me's to keep up with. The trouble with trying to to recreate oneself is either knowing when to settle on one personality or just continuing to take on more and more until you are so lost you can't remember who you are supposed to be. So all your feelings are in doubt because you are really just acting out a part. I'm pretty sure I've gone insane. I just don't have the energy anymore to keep it all going.

The writer sees a pathetic man and has no way of knowing, save for the complexity of the moods that flush across his face, in which man is the one that will prevail. The man sees the writer and smiles at his smugness. He is just another player. This goes nowhere. If the scene were to end or pause, what would all the player do? Who would they be? Are their lives complex? What do they believe in? Do they live good lives?

There must be one of me worth saving. I cannot see it now. So many starts. Not many good finishes.

This feels like the last bad finish yet it leaves so much undone.

FEELING VERY BAD

Well, as I've thought about it over the course of the day, I'm so conflicted I can hardly function. I just want to crawl into a hole and die. How can I be so off in all my thinking?

I guess I've put myself here. I'm not sure of anything right now. I think I'm trying to build something. It keeps calling. I keep building. I'm just too impulsive. I get something in my mind and I seize it because I know my mind will change soon or fail altogether.

This may be a turning point. Well, it is a turning point. I just wish I could settle my mind and just work.

TOO MUCH STUFF

Well, you seem to have a lot of projects again. Why not this year try to get rid of everything you know you won't fix up or can't. Seems like a lot of trouble. I've not been feeling well and I'm not so anxious to do all the things I wanted to do. Gotta let go of some stuff! Lot of emotional stuff tied to the physical stuff. It would be great to get rid of some of that, too.

Wow, I've actually had a moment of calm. I'm scared of dying and I feel like I'm dying or am about to. Perhaps it's time to calm down. God, I'm confused. Sometimes I want to die and then I see something or remember something and just can't bear it.

ALONE AGAIN

And in moments of madness
When I just want to scream
And the dreams I have had
Turned to dust down this road
And it seems like I'm travelin'
Alone again.

No one I know can live with me
Love with me, be with me for long
Before I find a way to be
Alone again.

I'M NOT MY OWN SELF ANYMORE

I'm not my own self anymore
I'm someone else
But I don't know who
I gave it all away
To a dream gone bad
And I'm someone else
And I don't know who
Which way's the way back
To where I need to be
And is that way
The way back to you
If I found you again
Would you know who I am
Cause I'm not my own self anymore
I'm someone else
Maybe you know who
It's hard to find a way
Back from nowhere else
When you're someone else
And you don't know who.

A SPOILED, LAZY MAN

I'm just a spoiled, lazy man
I've trained myself that way it seems
Maybe from a long time ago
I've shunned the hard times
Dulled my senses and carried on
With myself as if I had
A long time to go
I've done all the things I shouldn't have
And all of them more than once
I've said all the words I couldn't have
Followed up on for very long
If I had that long to go
And now that man that's been haunting
Me has showed up here and
He's taunting me
And if I had any time to go
All I'd want to do
Is show my love to you
But I'm running more to get away
From the darkness that seems sure to stay in me
And if I stood up to him face to face would there even be a trace of me
Of the man whose happy heart you gave
A reason to be free
I can see the saga of the road
It's deeper meanings coming clear
But it seems so hard
Not to be afraid
To look ahead with weathered eyes
And then hit the wall
While you're looking in the rear view mirror
There must be irony in here somewhere
But that and you have cleared the air
Thank you for always showing my best side.

FEELIN' PRETTY DOWN

I'm feeling pretty down
The things I've ignored
And tried to keep quiet
Are raging inside me
Spilling over to riot
Out of control spinning
Out and rolling
Over and over
It just won't stop
Over and over again
And I can't face
The things I've done
Or the reasons behind
All the lies that I've lived
The reaction to lies told to me
In this moment of dying
It's hard to reflect
But harder still not to
Could you have your way
Will you still
I've been feelin' pretty down
Wonderin' about a heart attack
Wonderin' about that the hell I lack inside
To let myself fall this far
Far away from where
All my dreams are waiting
They're just there waiting and
I still can't find my way.

DOWN TO DOWN, OUT TO OUT

There is no way around
The monster I gave life to
He's brought me down to down
And out to out
And taken most of everything
That I ever thought I loved
The only thing he's given me
Is a long and painful stare
At a life that's brought me
Down to down
And out to out and
Left me standin' sideways
In a field of "Never Gonna Be There"
Anyway so what's the point in standin'
You'll never be able to find your way
Thru this crooked path alone
But then who to trust
With this heart that's tattered
Who to trust with the last
Song that I'll ever sing alone
A man can die of a broken heart
And you're just a mirror
Of the life I took from you
And I just can't be face to face.

I'VE BEEN WANTING TO DIE

I've been wanting to die
For days on end
I can't explain the feelings now
They are scattered in the wind
I fear this time it's going to take me
I've fallen hard on these hard times
I've been waiting for someone to wake me
And tell me it's not true
This nightmare living in my heart
Is awfully dark it's awfully blue
My mom and I are very close on this
And on this we do agree
That more days than not we can't figure out
Why we should even be
There is no reason for us
Nobody cares and we
Fall into this void
There is no way out
Save for time
But more time means
More pain means more
Climbing inside deeper
To hide so why not die.

CLOSE TO THE EDGE

I feel like I'm close
To the edge of the light
But I'm still stumblin'
And rumblin' round
In the dark
I can't leave here
To be alone somewhere else
And I can't stay so alone
But the dawning light
Won't come to me
And I can't see
The road I'm on.

MADNESS

It's taking away the things I love
One by one they're falling
My heart is so raw
My nerves are shot
I can barely hear the calling
Of the ones who love me
They're somewhere far above me
And falling as I am
The voices fade into the night
My heart is so raw
By what right do I have
To fall at all.

SPINNING OUT AGAIN

Jesus would you look at me now
Spinnin' out again
I thought I got a long ways
Down this road
But it seems like it's over
I can't see the lines
It's dark up ahead
And I just can't find my way
 Lord if I give my life to you
Will you give it back to me
Will you take away this frightened man
Will you show me how to take a stand
Will you keep me from spinning' out like this
If I give my life to you
Can you show me where my heart has gone
Can you lead it back to me
I know that's a lot of questions
From a tired and lonely soul
But I gotta find the answers
Cause I'm spinnin' out again.

JUST 3 DAYS BEFORE THE FALL

I'm feeling pretty down
The things I've ignored
Are raging inside me
Spilling over to riot
Out of control, spinning out
And rolling over and over
It just won't stop
Over and over again
And I can't face
The things I've done
Or the reasons behind
All the lies I've lived
My reactions to the
Lies told to me
In this moment of dying
It's hard to reflect
But harder still not to
Could you have found your way
Could you still
I've been feeling pretty down
Wondering about a heart attack
Wondering about what the hell
I lack inside me
To let me fall this far
Far away from where
All my dreams are waiting
And still I can't find my way
There is no way around
The monster I gave life to
He's brought me down to down
And out to out, and taken
Most everything I loved
The only thing he's given me
Is a long and painful stare
At a life that's brought me
Down to down and out to out and
left me standing sideways
In a field of never gonna be there
So what's the point of standing
You'll never find your way back
Through this crooked path alone
And who would you trust

With this heart so tattered
Who to trust with the last song
That I'll ever sing alone
A man can die of a broken heart
And the mirror shows the life
That was taken from me
The mirrors image is
All that remains.

BACK FROM TREATMENT

A new life unfolding
I find myself holding
Back on some dreams
The muddy water it seems
Needs to clear a bit more

I'll look to the moment
To savor this time
To fall to my knees
The fear of what could be
Is replaced with what is
There's no time to fear time
As I look to this moment

If you're here in this moment
You can't run and hide
There's no need to fear
As you quicken your stride
And you're here in this moment
There's no fear in the moment at hand.

AIRTIGHT

It is quite warm
Here, where I sit
This early morn
Outside, winter
Is with us
At last for some
Alas for others
The snow has been
Trying all this day
And all the evening too
Cover the ground, she repeated
I will make soft everything
That pleases your eye
White, bright, it cleanses
Deeper and deeper does it drift
Objects on the ground bulge
From beneath the white depths
A new world unfolds
To be admired as beauty
Beyond description
Still, it is quite warm
Here, where I sit
This early morn.

ROLL WITH THE PUNCHES

You gotta roll with the punches
And let them think that you're a clown
You gotta roll with the punches
Cause one will always knock you down
You gotta roll with the punches
Man I'm here to tell ya' now
That if you roll with the punches
You'll just roll right back around

You never want to run away
You gotta stand and have your say
Then listen to the other side
It's usually just about your pride
Think of ways to smooth it out
Relax your tone and cease to shout
But if the other side won't give
Times a wastin' you gotta life to live

So you gotta roll with the punches
Let them think that you're a clown
You gotta roll with the punches
Cause one will always knock you down
You gotta roll with the punches
Man I'm here to let you know
That if you roll with the punches
You'll just roll right back around

And so you might resolve to stay
And put these wars aside
And live your life a better way
And put away your foolish pride
And learn to roll with the punches
Cause one will always knock you down
But if you roll with the punches
You'll just roll right back around.

THE STRAINS OF SOBRIETY

The Strains of Sobriety seem awfully hard to bear from the lofty flights of fantasy I've dreamed. Being present in the moment and quiet enough to care about a life I could not manage and those I loved who seemed to stand there, helpless as I fractured, eyes filled with tears, not knowing where to turn to or turn away from all the fears.

And now I stand here naked to the bone, most secrets revealed, lies stripped away, afraid to move forward for what has been shown as the pale frail man I was to the man that I could be, if only that my honesty could take me, shake me and set me free.

THE LONG ROAD BACK FROM HELL

It's a hard road you've chosen
This long road back from hell
It's a steep hollow climb up the hill
But you seem to be makin' it
Yeah, you're doing well
And your heart that was achin'
Is mending and your worried mind
Is finally beginning to
Still.

WALKIN' THE RIGHT ROAD

This is gonna take
Some getting used to
This is gonna take
A lot of fire in your heart
And if you don't take
The right road this time
You better get used to
Fallin' apart
Now walkin' the right road
Ain't that easy
You always gotta find a way
To stand your ground
But then you gotta move on
Slow and easy
While the rest of the world
Is just standing around
It might just take a little more than I got now
It may take a little bit
More than
That.

I STILL CAN'T SEE WHERE I'M COMING FROM

I've got a deep distaste for most folk
And I'm tolerant of some
I hide behind a rage so blind
I can't see where I'm comin' from
The walls are closin' in around me
And it's hard for me to breathe
The re-run of my life so far
Haunts me deeply and I grieve
It's a grieving for a lot of others
It's a wanting for this pain to end
It's a craving for the life that could have been
And ignorin' the life I'm about to end.
Like I said before as I closed that door
I'm hidin' behind a rage so blind
That I might appear to some
As a man so hard he's about to snap
And I still can't see where I'm comin' from
No I still can't see where I'm comin' from
So I'll wander thru this fantasy
That let's me write these words
And pour my heart to paper for a song
And I still can't help but wonder
Why I've been hangin' here so long
When I suddenly seem so out of place
Why it suddenly seems I've been so wrong
God help me find any way along this path.

DRINKING IS A SAD AFFAIR

Drinking is a sad affair
We do it and we just don't care
We drink and all our cares are gone
Literally all our cares are gone
The care we have for ourselves
The ones we love
The care we have for the day done well
A few drinks it goes all to hell
Better keep your head now.

TRUTH

Truth as a weapon is useless.
It is too naked.
Too raw.
Too destructive.
Yet as a tool
Might it not be tempered
To it's most
Productive End.

The Strength

An Honest Conversation with Dean

When did life really start to go down the rabbit hole of drug and alcohol addiction for you Dean?

In 1996 we put our business up For Sale with plans for a simpler life but abruptly, the sale went very badly and ended up in a lawsuit costing us our life savings. I slid once again into depression, drinking, pot and cocaine.

I bred rage, caressed resentment and stepped over the ragged edge of self defeat, after all I was entitled to this outrage, I had been wronged! I had been singled out by those who would do me harm and what harm they did! For how could people be so cold, so wanton, so greedy? Certainly I had the moral high ground here and I could prove it by the pathetic existence that I chose for myself. They would see what they had done to another human being! I would be an example, the perfect victim.

But to be that perfect victim takes a lot of work. One must have a place to hide, once must have a partner so self absorbed that my behavior would go unnoticed or if noticed, ignored outright. One must have a steady supply of money to spend in bars. One must have a drug dealer who could be called at any hour to fulfill my wants and needs. One must have a history of depression to fall back on if ever questioned seriously about one's behavior. It would all add up to a very nicely wrapped package of pity.

Ahhh, the fuel of the victim! Pity is like a salve. A bar is the perfect place for pity to flourish, or so it seems. The fellow on the next bench may listen to every word you say and acknowledge the very unfairness that brought you here. If you happen to buy him another beer, he'll listen all the more and nod his head knowingly as you tell your sad tale.

But at the end of the night, you still drive home alone to sleep it off and awaken to that gut wrenching fear that all the horrible things you proclaimed the night before are really true. And I believe today with certainty that I believed they were all true and thus I justified my burgeoning alcoholism, drug addiction and clinical depression.

The thought that I may be able to control any of these conditions I'm sure was still in my mind but the time had not yet come to exercise that option. It would always be there if I needed it.

But over the course of 6 years I fell deeper and deeper into the illusion that it really was everyone else's fault and I had no blame. I wasn't hurting anyone. I was just going off by myself, minding my own business because obviously no one really cared. Truth is, I'm the only that didn't care.

And you found yourself harboring suicidal thoughts?

Oh yes. There have been several times in my life where I thought the end was near. These times were usually preceded by my giving up on myself and falling victim to selfishness of the worse kind. For self pity is one of the darkest, tightest, loneliness boxes one can put oneself in and mind you in my experience, no one else can do it to us. It is self inflicted. However wallowing in this place can become tiresome and even for the most dedicated victim, one must rise. And rise I did! And I would tackle life again full of enthusiasm, big ideas and vast proclamations of love only to shatter that illusion again. Each time it became harder to rebound. And each time became deeper and darker.

On the day of your last drink, did you **know** *it was the day of your last drink?*

No.

My last drink was Sunday night, Sept. 28th, 2003. I had been listening to live music at the local tavern enjoying myself I'm sure and upon driving myself home at 2:30 in the morning, I blacked out on a curve and woke with someone pounding on the window of my truck. "Are you alright? Are you alright?" I looked up and around and saw that my truck was in a ditch head first. I quickly surmised that I could simply back out of this ditch and drive home.

The fellow at my window thought this to be a bad idea but I could not be persuaded and followed through on my plan. Waking up the next morning and only remembering bits and pieces of the night before, I finally knew that it was time to stop.

I was miserable no matter what I did. If I drank, I was miserable. If I didn't drink I was miserable. If I smoked pot, I was miserable. If I didn't, I was miserable. If I talked to anyone, I was miserable. If no one was there to talk to, I was miserable.

This went on for a week at the end of which time my broken brain decided that I should go down to my boat, sail out to the middle of the Puget Sound, turn on the propane, light a match and disappear into the mist. How romantic would that be! A statement. How could I be blamed? I would be thanked for ending the misery that I had caused everyone.

Finally a practical solution with a fair chance of success! I had not seen success for quite sometime and the chance was seductive.

On the way to my boat that day, I passed a sign that said "Hospital" and for the briefest moment I thought, "What if?" And as if God's hand took the wheel, I followed the sign.

So I drove to the emergency ward, went to the front desk and told them I needed help and burst into tears. I was still sobbing as they checked me into the psychiatric ward and for the following three days.

On the fourth day, a meeting was held between myself, the doctor and my wife. He informed her that I was a late stage alcoholic with liver damage, I was a drug addict and I was clinically depressed. He expressed the difficulties ahead recovering from just one or two of these addictions, let alone all three. I remember the shock on my wife's face. Had she not realized what was going on with all this time?

She left.

They signed me up to go to a 28 day Alcohol Recovery Program at a local rehab facility.

Thus began the start of a new and unrealized life.

How horrible is de-tox? What does one go through? How long does it take?

Well, first would be the psychological effects. For me, just getting out of a psych ward of a local hospital and being transported immediately to this treatment center, I didn't know which way was up. I was still harboring the idea that I could do this on my own, I really wasn't that sick, I was just tired. Maybe this rehab place would give me the opportunity to rest up and figure things out.

There was a 72 hour black out where I wasn't allowed to call anyone or receive any calls and I was pretty much isolated from the rest of the facility.

The isolation gave me an opportunity to think about what I was doing. Unfortunately, being a late stage alcohol and drug addict curtailed my ability to think clearly. I was grateful for three days of just chilling out.

The physical effects of those first three days were not what one might expect for a late stage alcoholic. I did not have D.T.'s, I wasn't hallucinating and my body wasn't wracked with pain. I think I just felt numb all over.

It had been two weeks since I had a drink and I don't think that I felt like I *needed* one but I sure as hell *wanted* one.

When the 72 hours had ended, I was given a room, my schedule, my counselor and my homework assignments. I guess this was the real start of the treatment program but I didn't like the idea of homework or studying. I still thought that if they just gave me a book, I could just read it and figure it out on my own.

Just what exactly IS Recovery?

I didn't really understand what a program of recovery was. I kept thinking, "Recovery from *what?*" still denying that I may have a drinking problem.

Footnote: *It's amazing to what extent the ego will go to convince us we are who we think we are rather than who we really are.*

During the first week of my recovery program, I was still deeply in denial. I was ashamed, I was angry, bitter, resentful and filled with hate for all those who had done me wrong and made me end up here. I just kind of walked around in a daze looking at the tops of my shoes unable to look anyone in the eye, not wanting to hear what anyone said, still isolated.

Somewhere during the second week I noticed that some of my recovery associates were more cheerful, more positive and seemed to be *getting it*. Some were excited by the possibility of never having to drink again. I still wasn't ready to let go of that.

And then one day I raised my head and looked someone in the eye. Amazingly they looked back in my eyes and we started a conversation. What did I want to get out of this? What did they want to get out of this? Was what we wanted anything like what we were getting? Or was it a complete surprise?

The answers were slow to come. But over the remaining two weeks, the fact that those around me were actively seeking recovery finally convinced me that I could let go of this notion that I could do it all myself. I realized that I had been fighting my entire life. Not sure what I was fighting for anymore but still, needing to fight. It all seemed so silly.

Laying in my bunk one night I finally decided to just let go and asked God for help. I had surrendered. I had acknowledged the first step in Alcoholics Anonymous: *We admitted that we were powerless over alcohol, that our lives had become unmanageable.*

I was a bit relieved! I said it out loud. I listened to the words, they bounced around in my head a little bit and I thought, "My God, this might be possible after all."

That was a turning point for me. I studied and I

talked in group therapy. I talked with other patients. I went to the meetings held at the center and was even asked to chair some of the meetings.

In as much as I had noticed other people *getting it* early on in recovery, it seemed now that some of the newcomers were telling me that I was *getting it*. It was the first time in awhile that I began to believe something positive about myself.

After all, the whole idea of recovery is not to stop drinking, it's to learn to live without alcohol. I am still an alcoholic, my goal is just to not act like one.

Does being an addict just mean one is weak of character?

Well, I always believed that to be true. However in A.A. parlance, I was the poster boy for the John Wayne Handbook of living. I envisioned myself with a strong and true character. Apparently, that was not the case.

It seems that alcoholism and drug addiction have little or nothing to do with strength of character. In fact, we are asked to let go of what we have imagined our character to be for that very character brought us to the doors of recovery.

While in treatment I learned that alcoholism is truly a disease. Some of us are predisposed to it through genetics. Have you ever noticed some people in a social gathering actually leaving a half full glass on the table and walking away? I could never understand that. But then I'm an alcoholic. I would go get that glass and finish it. It had nothing to do with my character. It was just my alcoholic behavior acting out its role.

How do I talk to somebody about stopping their drug or alcohol use?

There are many resources available to learn the process of talking with an alcoholic. Al-Anon is often recommended for those who have been affected by alcoholism in their loved ones and friends. It is also said that to have lived with an alcoholic long term, one may be affected in a negative way and be unable to talk with an alcoholic constructively.

I had family and friends try to talk to me for years. I always blew it off as "just relaxing", unwinding after a hectic day. How can I have a drinking problem just drinking beer with an occasional scotch chaser? Even as I approached the breaking point, I couldn't admit that I was an alcoholic and whoever tried to convince me of such had to be an idiot. They didn't know me. They didn't know what pain I had gone through. How could they understand what a man like me felt? If they had known, they would understand why I drank.

There is no doubt in my mind that anyone you know who is having a problem with drinking also knows someone who is in recovery. I've been taught that as an alcoholic, recovery *will not come* unless we want it to. It will not come if we do it for our wives nor will it come if we do it keep our jobs nor will it come to save our houses, our cars, our family and life as we know it until we are convinced that there is no other way, until we have been laid so low that there is nothing in us left to object to a new start. Only then can we become willing to look at life anew and accept and admit that we may have been wrong, that we may have indeed lost our way and long to live again.

In your experience, what is an addict's biggest fear?

To me there was no biggest fear. It was the fear of everything. The fear of being discovered while I snuck off to smoke a joint or someone catching me laying out a line of cocaine or being seen leaving the tavern drunk by someone I respected. Fear is almost the catalyst that enables an alcoholic to remain an alcoholic. To me fear was the fuel that kept my martyrdom burning bright, the ultimate victim. It was much easier for me to fear something than to deal with it and accept it. The fear was long term. I could wallow in it for as long as I could be the victim.

Being a victim of course has its own rewards. There are those who will feel sorry for you and never confront you head-on with the truth about you. Yes, the truth. I thought I had everybody fooled. The truth was not something I was familiar with. It wasn't useful. I had no way of obtaining what I needed using anything close to the truth. Truth, in the end, was what I feared most for ultimately truth was the light that I feared. Darkness was my friend and we had no affection for honesty.

Seriously, if someone is completely down and out, totally addicted and at the end of their rope, how does one ask for help when they have absolutely nothing left?

It's very hard to know. I wish I had the answer that could help everyone escape that dark prison. I don't have that answer. All I can do as an alcoholic is talk about how it was for me, what happened, and how it is now. If only one word of my story resonated with someone and gave them pause, perhaps it would give them the first glimpse of the journey back to life.

However, the sad truth is there are a lot of people that don't get the message of recovery. In every corner of the world today, there are thousands suffering from alcoholism, drug addiction, addictions of all kinds. Though help does exist in all corners of the world, few are able to find it without some form of spiritual experience, keeping in mind everyone's unique belief in their spirituality.

For me it was Step 2 in Alcoholics Anonymous: "Came to believe that a power greater than ourselves can restore us to sanity."

I was fortunate in many ways. I fought through five life events of utter desperation, desolation and the possibility of dying. With each event came some miniscule shred of hope. I have no idea where it came from and I had no formula for conjuring it up. It was just something stronger than me that gave me a glimpse of hope, just enough hope to wait another second and in that second, perhaps salvation, and in thinking about salvation, came another second or two.

The Hope

THE HOPE

I am most grateful for the help I have received in the last 10 years of my life. I am told that I have become a genuinely good person. I suppose an example would be that 10 years ago no one would have trusted me to walk their dog. Today I have the privilege of being handed the keys to a school bus and the responsibility of transporting preschool children who bring me more joy than I ever thought possible.

Many other wonderful things have become possible through sobriety. To me, one of the most important is being able to love unconditionally to the best of my understanding and being able to receive love unconditionally to the best of my understanding. And with that my understanding grows each day.

Love is a self fulfilling prophecy. As long as I let it be, don't judge, don't expect, don't resent, don't fool myself or my love, today I get to experience the gift of love. In the end, for me, not much else matters. It seems to carry me where ever I go and with whomever I come into contact.

Keep in mind these are lofty and only partially true claims and in reality there are days that I let down my guard and start to dwell in my head. That's where most of the problems seem to be. I can imagine all sorts of things, good, bad and indifferent if left to my own devices.

Relief from that seems to be giving back to those who have suffered much the same as I have.

What is The Hope?

Simply put, the hope is another day of sobriety. That day is dependent upon my spiritual condition, my physical condition and my emotional condition. If all of these are in sync and I am using the tools that I have been given in sobriety then I stand a fair chance of making it through another day without drinking or taking drugs.

Hope for those who are still suffering can be found

at times in simply being willing to ask for help. The first time I sincerely asked for help I was awestruck by the emotions it evoked. It was like something in me admitting that I may have been wrong and for the first time, that confession seemed to be okay. For some reason the will of my ego was powerless over the willingness to live anew.

I've thought a lot about my will versus God's will. My will nearly destroyed my life on several occasions. My determination to find the answer to my problems through sheer force of will always ended badly. It just seems to me that willingness, when applied to *anything*, opens the door to possibilities that with an inspired motive can produce marvelous results.

If one remains willing and hopeful, the light may be nearer than previously thought.

If you could reach out to someone struggling with alcohol or drugs, what's the first thing you would do?

There is a chapter in the big book of Alcoholics Anonymous that goes directly to the heart of this question. It's Chapter 7, "Working with Others". I would not attempt to approach an individual by myself. I would take along my A.A. sponsor. It seems to be a delicate balance between sharing our experience and listening. It's useless to try to convince someone that they should stop and if we get too involved in A.A. dogma, it can often turn that person away. As has been stated previously, that person *has to want* to become sober, there is no other way.

I have seen people court ordered to A.A. meetings just going through the motions, never really listening and never sharing. They just get their slip signed and are the first out the door. It seems they don't really think they have a problem. I've heard people say that they're seeking recovery as a last straw to save their marriage. It seems that is a blind alley as well.

But quite often I hear stories from people who have lost their wives and family, lost their jobs, lost their houses, lost their drivers licenses, lost their dignity and have turned to A.A. for help. These are the ones that have resigned to do *anything it takes* for sobriety. They don't seem to be looking to regain their former place in society; they just want out from under the pain and the shadow of alcoholism and drug addiction. These folks stand a pretty good chance of staying sober today. To keep that fire alive in them, they must practice tomorrow everything they do today, all of which is preceded by willingness.

How much does God, religion and/or spirituality play into Recovery even for a person who is not a "Believer"?

I have never considered myself to be a religious person. I have never attended church on anything like a regular basis. I was baptized in a congregational church. In my twenties, I dabbled with Buddhism, Catholicism and several New Age movements that were the religion du jour. I always felt that there was something very special that was watching over all of us. Many times in my life, I've had what I call 'spiritual experiences'. I don't know how else to define them other than miraculous things happening when all hope seemed to be gone. But as I think of it, it was always when I stopped so hard trying to figure it out on my own and asked for help.

For those that may be looking for help, I don't think it matters one way or another what your religion is, what your spiritual beliefs may be or that you have religious or spiritual beliefs at all.

A.A. does talk about God. In fact, Step 3 is "made a decision to turn our will and our lives over to the care of God (as we understood him)". When I first heard this in treatment, I kind of felt relieved. It didn't put me in a categorized religion, it didn't single me out as religious, spiritual, atheistic or agnostic. It was just a simple statement that I didn't have to ponder and get sidetracked by the dogma. I was comfortable enough with that to accept it. They also refer to it as a "power greater than ourselves". I suppose the key there is admitting that there may be something greater than ourselves, our ego, greater than our will, greater than all the justification we had to muster to put us in treatment to begin with.

It was also probably my first glimpse of honesty.

If you could help change lives with one word, what would that word be?

Honesty.

Boy there's a word that I never really understood. I always thought I was honest. I could make the correct change in a transaction, if a clerk gave me too much change, I gave it back. I think they refer to that as "cash register honesty" but that is far from the honesty that I have learned in sobriety.

That honesty is what ultimately saved me.

It is simply having the courage to face myself without the filter of all the justifications I needed to be a victim of my own devices.

As a practicing alcoholic, honesty was not all that useful. It rarely got me the sympathy that I needed or rarely got me the attention I craved, albeit negative, and the pity that kept me believing that I was such a tortured soul.

What seemed to make all the difference to me in early sobriety was Step 4 in Alcoholics Anonymous, "Made a searching and fearless moral inventory of ourselves". Good God! Who the hell would want to do that? Well, I was in hell so I figured I'd better do it. It was not easy. Most things in my inventory were certainly not things that I would admit to anyone else and some to the extent that I couldn't admit to myself. But there it was in stark reality, "HONESTY". Once I dug into this inventory and started to uncover some of my motives in life that had brought me to my knees, I began to see a pattern and with each new confession another would open up.

It took me a long time to do it. I've seen other folks do it in one sitting. I've also seen people take four years to do it. It took me 4 months and a lot of encouragement from my sponsor.

Finally, I was ready for the next step. Step 5,

"Admitted to God, to ourselves and to another human being the exact nature of our wrongs". This is where the rubber meets the road. It seems that any exclusions remain secrets and any secret that I was not willing to expose remained a distraction. If questioned, I would either have to justify, lie, omit or just ignore. It seemed to me that would put me right back where I started. I read the Step again and it indeed said, "a *searching and fearless* moral inventory", not the evasive and half hearted inventory I would have done in my past.

Thus my first brush with honesty was difficult and yet the most rewarding thing I've ever experienced. Having completed Step 5, I had nothing left to hide. I was free! Nobody had anything over me, I didn't have to worry about what lies I had to tell what people, I didn't have to look over my shoulder for the lies I have told, it was all out there. God. What a relief!

How do you get over guilty feelings of things that happened in the past as part of moving forward?

I'm not sure I've gotten over them yet. But I've sure looked at them - *honestly*. With each one, I had to be willing to accept my part and take responsibility for what I had done regardless of circumstances. Had someone wronged me and had I retaliated? I had to face the possibility that I may have manifested that wrong done to me. And at the time being unwilling to be honest with myself, I had retaliated only to soothe my ego and ignore my part. In Steps 6, 7 and 8 of the A.A. big book, it starts with, "we were entirely ready to have God remove all these defects of character". Step 7 is "humbly asked him to remove our short comings". Step 8 says "made a list of all persons we had harmed and became willing to make amends to them all".

The next step was the hard part for me. All the words on the page are just fine until there is a call for action and this one was action of a kind that would require a lot of support from my sponsor and my fellow A.A.

members. It was Step 9, "made direct amends to such people where ever possible except when to do so would injure them or others." This was not something to be taken lightly.

In the early years of my sobriety, I did the best that I could making amends to family, loved ones, associates and employers. But there were and still are those that I haven't made. Some because I may be one of the others that would be so injured.

I guess an important point to make here is that this is a process. Rather than get too hung up on deeds of days gone by, I try to make sure that today, this day, I hope not to drink. I don't create further need to make amends to anyone.

Step 10 says, "Continued to take personal inventory and when we were wrong, promptly admitted it." It sounds easy enough. But sometimes if I'm caught up in the heat of a discussion and it seems more important to make my point than to concede another's, admitting I was wrong is the farthest thing from my mind. I don't always have the presence of mind to admit that I am wrong. And at times the word 'promptly' to my alcoholic brain says soon, in awhile, later, *whatever*.

But in the end, I know I was wrong and if I let it stew in my head, it will become a *thing*. If I am to stay healthy in body, mind and spirit, I cannot allow such things to stay in my head. If they hadn't meant 'promptly', they would not have written it as such.

In Step 11, it helps us out a little bit with this. (It's one of my favorite Steps, I do my best to practice it before I go to bed and when I wake up in the morning and it sure doesn't hurt to think about it several times a day). "Sought through prayer and meditation to improve our conscious contact with God *as we understood him,* praying only for knowledge of His will for us and the power to carry that out".

How do you like *yourself again?*

It's taken awhile. As we have discussed previously, this is a process which requires that we follow the Steps. They seem to be put in a natural order.

I guess the final Step, Step 12 is the one that gave me the most hope for ever liking myself again. In a way it promised that if I stayed spiritually, emotionally and physically healthy, I would have a daily reprieve from the disease of alcoholism.

"Having had a spiritual awakening as the result of these Steps, we try to carry this message to alcoholics, and to practice these principles in all of our affairs."

Taken as a whole, this can seem to a fairly daunting task and as such is discussed in great detail in the big book of Alcoholics Anonymous, however; taken one at a time and understood one at a time, the progression to the next step seems perfectly natural.

And for me, it was perfectly natural. For the life I had lived for 55 years literally brought me to deaths door. I realized I had practiced dying most of my life. Suddenly sobriety had given me a life I had never known. If I was willing to take direction and do what was asked of me to remain sober, this new life was mine to keep.

And I wanted to get really good at it!

If you can tell people the most important thing you have learned in this experience, what would it be?

All I can do is talk a little bit about what the most important things were to me. I think it's different for everyone.

I remember hearing early on that the only thing that you have to change in sobriety is *everything*. But weighing that against so many years of pain, heartbreak and desperation, it didn't seem too difficult a task. The only things I was really changing were the things that hurt me so badly and nothing about sobriety seemed to invoke any darkness at all. In fact, the light was radiant!

The concept of humility was another big one for me. Being humble. Accepting others for who and what they are, not judging, offering kindness. For me that is a process as well. I'm not used to accepting people. I spent a lot of years judging people. It was much easier for me to criticize and judge other people than to actually do anything myself and risk being judged and criticized. I became the consummate critic of life's common problems while refusing to accept life on life's terms. It seemed so much easier to envision a future so perfect, so far out of reach, so unreasonable to attain, that I could never succeed. By not succeeding, I could remain the victim.

I heard a fellow at a meeting one time say (with tongue in cheek), "I'm very humble. As a matter of fact, I am way more humble than most of you!" Funny? Yes. Humble? No.

It occurs to me that humility, although probably a state of mind, has more to do with my soul. I'm not at all sure why I think that, it's just a very strong feeling that I have. I don't always trust my state of mind, it has lied to me in the past and still many facets of it are in need of repair.

So I'm often in the habit of referring things to my heart, that nebulous place where the warm feelings come from and the feelings I'm unsure of are sent. I'm pretty sure my heart is nowhere near as cluttered as my mind. Perhaps as those feelings percolate in my heart, get stripped of all the white noise that exists around us, become warm with love and understanding, then it will feel safe enough to send them to my mind. Who knows.

I'm always going to be an alcoholic, there's no getting around it.

But in the end, I do not have to behave like one.

I have options.

I have people I can call to make sure that my mind is not off on a terror. I have meetings I can go to and listen to other people tell their stories, sometimes I even tell my story. There is always something I can do to keep myself from taking that first drink.

All I have to do is practice, practice, practice all

these principles in all my affairs.

You are publishing this book on September 28, 2013. Tell us about the meaning behind that.

It is 10 years to the day since I took my last drink.

At times it seems like its gone by very fast. I think of all the meetings that I've attended and all the wonderful people I've come to know. The support system and network that enables me to continue to be sober one day at a time is a testament to those A.A. pioneers in the early 1930's. I am honored to be a part of this group and to be able to give back what I have been given so graciously - Life.

So just a note to you, the reader, if you've made it this far through the book, my hat is off to you and I am grateful. Most of what I have learned and passed on in this book is information and insights gleaned from the ten years I have been sober and my association with Alcoholics Anonymous.

There's a fella' that I see quite frequently at meetings who has 52 years of sobriety. When asked to speak, without fail, he starts his dialogue with, "A.A. is not for those that need it; it's for those that want it."

Whether A.A. is for you or not is a question I can not answer.

What I can share is that I found in A.A. the tools that I needed to live successfully without alcohol and drugs, to believe in the power greater than myself and to embrace faith that everything is exactly as it should be in spite of me.

Sincerely,
Dean Ingram

For further information,
Please visit:

www.deaningram.com

www.facebook.com/ingrambooks

ingrambooks@yahoo.com

Made in the USA
San Bernardino, CA
10 March 2016